D1576486

Fifty Years of the Westerns

David Cross

First published 2012

ISBN 978 0 7110 3658 1

Published by Ian Allan Publishing

an imprint of Ian Allan Publishing Ltd, Hersham, Surrey, KT12 4RG
Printed in England by Ian Allan Printing Ltd, Hersham, Surrey KT12 4RG

Distributed in the United States of America and Canada by BookMasters Distribution Services

Visit the Ian Allan Publishing website at www.ianallanpublishing.com

Front cover: See page 58

Back cover: Happily seven 'Westerns' survive in preservation. Nowadays owned by the Western Locomotive Association, No D1062 *Western Courier* is normally based on the Severn Valley Railway but in 2009 visited the West Somerset Railway, being seen here on the afternoon of 14 June heading a uniform rake of chocolate-and-cream Mk 1 stock past Leigh Bridge en route from Minehead to Bishops Lydeard. *Don Bishop*

Previous page: Apparently fresh from overhaul, its fresh paint gleaming in the soft light of a late summer's evening, No D1052 *Western Viceroy* awaits departure from Westbury with a train for Plymouth. Unfortunately the date of the photograph is uncertain, although the mix of maroon and blue-and-grey Mk 1 stock suggests that it was taken in the late 1960s. *John Spencer Gilks*

Below: A photograph of a Western on the Highland Line! 19-21 June 2009 saw No D1015 Western Champion again travel to Scotland, this time complete with 'Western Chieftain' headboard. The special reached all the way to the west coast of Scotland at Kyle of Lochalsh. This picture was taken of the train setting off from Pitlochry. *Bob Avery*

Introduction

Fifty years! Can it really be so long since the first of the 'Westerns' emerged from Swindon Works? The following that these most elegant of diesel locomotives continue to enjoy is nothing short of remarkable, and in view of this it seems a pity that none was given the name *Western Endurance*! The history of the class will, of course, be familiar to many readers, but for the benefit of others a brief résumé is perhaps in order.

By 1959 the Western Region had identified a requirement for a more powerful diesel-hydraulic locomotive than the existing B-B 'Warship' design ('D8xx' series), which in its final form produced a total of 2,200hp from its twin Maybach engines, and in July of that year the British Transport Commission authorised construction of 74 locomotives of a new design. They were to perpetuate the stressed-skin construction principle of the 'Warships' and the use of two Maybach engines, but these were to be of the uprated MD655 type, each developing a nominal 1,350hp (giving a combined output of 2,700hp), driving through Voith (rather than Mekydro) transmission. However, the extra power was achieved by turbocharging, and the need to accommodate intercoolers and larger radiators resulted in a larger and heavier locomotive, dictating a C-C wheel arrangement. The final design was 68ft long, 9ft wide and 13ft 1in high and weighed 108 tons; maximum speed was 90mph. Its striking appearance was influenced by industrial designer and architect Misha (later Sir Misha) Black, working in consultation with members of the BR Design Panel, which was keen to avoid the 'nose-end' style of earlier diesels. The result was a highly distinctive locomotive – arguably the best-looking of BR's diesels.

Livery was also the subject of much debate, involving WR management, members of the BTC and the Design Panel, and the first locomotive, No D1000 *Western Enterprise*, appeared in December 1961 in a shade of beige, described as 'desert sand'. Others followed in green, maroon and, most bizarrely, golden ochre, which turned out to be an exact match for the shade that had been chosen in the late 19th century by William Stroudley for his locomotives on the London, Brighton & South Coast Railway. This would be confined to just one 'Western', but, perhaps surprisingly, the WR management spurned green in favour of maroon, and it was in this livery that the vast majority were placed in traffic; later all would succumb to the ubiquitous Rail blue.

Construction of the class was shared by the BR works at Swindon and Crewe, but by the time the last example (No D1029 *Western Legionnaire*) was turned out by Swindon in May 1964 the tide had turned against diesel-hydraulics. As a result the 'Westerns' – or Class 52s, as they became known following the introduction of BR's computerised classification scheme – were to have woefully short lives, the class remaining intact for just nine years. First to go were Nos D1019 *Western Challenger* and D1032 *Western Marksman*, condemned in May 1973, and the last survivors were withdrawn from BR service in February 1977.

During their BR careers the 'Westerns' were confined very largely to the Western Region, but the seven preserved examples are now to be found all over England: indeed, in recent years No D1015 *Western Champion* has even visited Scotland during the course of its exploits back on the main line. The others – Nos D1010 *Western Campaigner*, D1013 *Western Ranger*, D1023 *Western Fusilier*, D1041 *Western Prince*, D1048 *Western Lady* and D1062 *Western Courier* – have all worked on preserved lines and have dedicated preservation groups looking after them. Needless to say, the restoration of a large diesel locomotive does not come cheap; in 2011 members of the Western Locomotive Association, seeking to return *Western Courier* to main-line standards, voted unanimously to set up a fund to raise £120,000, of which around £80,000 will be needed to lift the body and attend to the bogies, the remainder to comply with modern safety requirements. Such work can be achieved only with the support of the enthusiast movement, and it is testimony to the enduring appeal of the 'Westerns' that this support has thus far been forthcoming.

So why, more than three decades after they were withdrawn by BR, are we still celebrating the 'Westerns'? What was it that made them so popular? Well, for their time they had a 'wow' factor in terms of appearance, size, the fact they were all named and perhaps because they were to be used on the former Great Western Railway, where front-line named passenger locomotives have always been held in the highest regard. I well recall my first encounter with the type, shared with my late father, Derek, at the bridge over the North Wales main line near Chester Golf Club, at Saltney; that afternoon, during August 1962, we saw the nose of No D1007 *Western Talisman* appear on the line from Wrexham, the first 'Western' either of us had ever seen, and we were both bowled over by the look of this brand-new diesel. I was so impressed that I managed to persuade Derek to go to Chester station the following day in case another 'Western' should turn up on the afternoon Paddington–Birkenhead service. Derek agreed, albeit reluctantly (stations were not his favourite places), and went on to mutter about how much more interesting a steam locomotive would have been. Either way, it had been a great day; earlier we had photographed Stanier Pacific No 46241 *City of Edinburgh* on the 'Irish Mail' to Holyhead. The following day No D1001 *Western Pathfinder* duly materialised, and I have been a fan of the class ever since. Even Derek, whose first love was, of course, steam, grew to like 'Westerns' a great deal, and he also took some very respectable photographs of the class during the course of their short working lives.

This book is a broad pictorial record of the class from 1961 to the present day; it does not attempt to feature each and every locomotive, which would, in any case, have been impossible, as a number seem to have been particularly camera-shy! The majority of the pictures are the work of my late father, and most are previously unpublished. Much of

Derek's material was taken either on Kodachrome 35mm film or on Agfa CT18 colour-negative film. Although Derek had a Linhof press camera, which took 120-size film, by the time many of these colour pictures were taken he was probably using his Rollei SL66 camera, again on 120 film, giving twelve 2¼x2¼in images per roll of film. The 35mm slides were taken on a variety of Leica and Canon 35mm cameras with either a fixed standard lens or a telephoto lens (a silver torpedo-shaped affair) – all, of course, in the days before modern zoom lenses. While on the subject of photography, it seems appropriate to record that, during the time this book has been in preparation, an era has come to a close with the decision at the end of 2010 by the little-known Dwayne's Photo Service, of Parsons, Kansas, to cease processing Kodachrome film, production of which had itself ceased the previous year. Introduced in 1935, this was the world's first and, arguably, most successful colour film, and it has lasted well; we all owe Kodak a debt of gratitude.

In concluding I should like to express my thanks to all those who have helped with the compilation of this book, notably John Spencer Gilks, Bob Kimmins (who now holds the collection of photographs taken by my friend Les Riley), Julian Peters (who has kindly allowed me to use some of the photographs taken by his late father, Ivo – a regular companion of Derek's on his West Country jaunts), Simon Dewey and Martin Shenton. Finally, I should like to thank my mother, for allowing my father the time to take these now historic photographs, and my wife, for her support and encouragement. I hope that you enjoy the result and that, for many of you, it brings back some happy memories.

David Cross
Brentwood

The 'Westerns' were always popular with traincrews, as these two smiling faces would appear to confirm. In the driving seat is Bescot driver Mark Dale, whilst standing in the doorway is Rotherham driver Richard Ainley; as the drivers' home depots might suggest, the picture is a recent one, taken *on 20 March 2010* at the unlikely location of Wakefield Kirkgate. By now, of course, No D1054 *Western Governor* was long gone, its memory being perpetuated by No D1015, temporarily renumbered and renamed for the day's 'Western Rocks' railtour from Bristol to Buxton. *Peter Sheppard*

No D1000 *Western Enterprise*, pristine in its unique 'desert sand' livery, stands outside Swindon Works shortly after completion in late 1961. It would enter traffic on 20 December on trials from Plymouth Laira depot, destined to become the spiritual home of the class. Note, beneath the number, the WR-style red spot denoting route availability. *Colour-Rail*

Above: Construction of the 'Westerns' was shared between Swindon and Crewe, which built more than half the class (Nos D1030-73). Completed earlier in the month, No D1037 *Western Empress*, immaculate in green livery with red name and number plates, tackles Hatton Bank – six miles at 1 in 100 between Warwick and Birmingham – in August 1962. Judging from the locomotive's condition this may well have been its first revenue-earning duty, although the clearly spurious reporting number disguises the train's identity and suggests a demonstration or crew-training run. *Colour-Rail*

Left: Green-liveried No D1003 *Western Pioneer* pauses at Taunton in August 1962 when less than four months old. Only seven 'Westerns' (Nos D1002-4/35-8) were introduced in green, which in the author's opinion suited them very well, although the more commonly held preference seems to be for maroon, which marked them out from most other contemporary Type 4s. The train is an up express, in all likelihood taking the 'Berks & Hants' line via Westbury and Newbury to Reading, some 106 miles distant, on its way to Paddington. *B. Arman/Colour-Rail*

Crewe-built No D1047 *Western Lord* was released to traffic in February 1963 and as part of its delivery run was used to haul a Class 4 inter-regional freight from Crewe as far as Wolverhampton, being pictured at Aldersley Road bridge, just short of Oxley Branch Junction. Here the locomotive would be replaced by a GWR 'Hall' steam locomotive and thence run light to the Western Region depot nearby at Oxley to be formally accepted by the WR. Allocated initially to Cardiff Canton, for hauling express passenger trains between London and South Wales, it would be withdrawn just 13 years later, in February 1976. *Doug Nicholson*

Illustrating the changeover from steam to diesel traction is this picture of a GWR Prairie tank, No 6169, on a short pick-up goods at Bicester North station on 17 February 1963. Approaching at speed is an unidentified maroon-liveried 'Western' with an express from Paddington to Wolverhampton Low Level. In the early 1960s, when electrification of the West Coast main line was in progress, this served as the principal route from London to the West Midlands, but its importance has since declined. However, at the time of writing (2012) plans are in hand to upgrade the line, whereby journey times between Bicester and London will reduced from 56 to 44 minutes. *John Spencer Gilks*

Deep inside Swindon Works stands green-liveried No D1004 *Western Crusader*. The locomotive, which had been built at Swindon and was released to traffic in May 1962, appears to have been used in service and had presumably returned for repairs that were too extensive for its home depot of Plymouth Laira to handle at the time; the photograph is believed to have been taken in the spring of 1963. No D1004 would have a working life of barely 11 years, being withdrawn in August 1973 and scrapped at Swindon in September 1974. *Martin Shenton*

Left: Although the 'Western' was a product of the Design Office at Swindon and is regarded as a quintessentially Western Region diesel-hydraulic locomotive, it is sometimes forgotten that nearly 60% of the class were actually built at Crewe. Moreover, photographs of 'Westerns' at Crewe Works are much less common than those taken at Swindon, so it is particularly pleasing to be able to include this picture of Nos D1071 *Western Renown* and D1070 *Western Gauntlet* nearing completion at Crewe in September 1963, in company with a couple of English Electric Type 4 (Class 40) locomotives in for repair. *Western Gauntlet* would be placed in traffic in October 1963 from Cardiff Canton, *Western Renown* entering service the following month from Old Oak Common depot in London. *Martin Shenton*

Left: Another view of the 'Western' production line at Crewe Works in September 1963, showing a further three examples largely complete and in undercoat. The identities of the locomotives are not clear but could be from the series D1030-4, which although numerically 'early' were in fact the last locomotives to be completed, the original intention having been that these locomotives would be built at Swindon. No D1034 *Western Dragoon* (rather than No D1073, as might have been expected) was thus the final Crewe-built example to be placed in traffic, in April 1964 from Bristol Bath Road depot. *Martin Shenton*

This fine photograph, taken during the summer of 1965, features No D1051 *Western Ambassador* calling at Shrewsbury with a train from Birkenhead to Paddington via Chester, Wrexham and Wolverhampton Low Level. By this time demolition of the overall roof was well underway, but the station at Shrewsbury remains a fascinating place, not least on account of the station building itself, built in 1848 in Tudor style, reputedly to match the Tudor buildings of Shrewsbury School. The station is now Grade II listed, as is the LNWR 1903-built signalbox, which very distinctive structure, 100ft long, 30ft high and 12ft wide, is the largest manual signalbox still in use in the UK. *Martin Shenton*

Saturday 31 July 1965 finds an immaculate maroon No D1031 *Western Rifleman* creeping past Severn Tunnel Junction station with a westbound parcels train. To the west of the tunnel, about a mile away and through which the train has just passed, is one of the most sustained gradients (three miles at 1 in 90) on the main line to South Wales. The passenger station here remains open, but the extensive yards that could be found at this location are, sadly, no more, and the land to the far right of the picture has been redeveloped as the toll-booth area for the new Severn Crossing. *John Spencer Gilks*

On 2 July 1966 an unidentified 'Western' passes through Exeter St Thomas station, a mile or so to the west of St Davids, with a Motorail service from Kensington Olympia to Newton Abbot. From here the train will pass through Exminster and Starcross, thereafter following the coastline as it passes through Dawlish Warren, Dawlish and Teignmouth *en route* to its destination, 20 miles away. At the time of the photograph it would have comprised around eight passenger coaches and a number of 'carflats' carrying the passengers' cars. Such trains were very popular at the height of the holiday season, serving, over the years, Newton Abbot, Plymouth, St Austell and Penzance. Exeter St Thomas station remains open today, albeit much changed, being served by local services between Exeter and the far West. *John Spencer Gilks*

Right: Heading a Summer Saturday express on 14 August 1966, a dirty maroon 'Western' (believed to be No D1042 *Western Princess*, though this is not confirmed) passes Blatchbridge Junction, at the south end of the Frome avoiding line. Also known as the Frome cut-off, this was opened in 1933 to speed the journey to/from the West Country, the other end of the line being at Clink Road Junction. Visible in the background is the original line, serving Frome. *John Spencer Gilks*

Below: Maroon-liveried No D1009 *Western Invader* accelerates away from the Newton Abbot stop and towards Aller Junction on 12 June 1969. The train is the 14.30 Paddington–Penzance, comprising a uniform rake of blue-and-grey stock. Most carriages carry the large yellow destination boards that were used for a time in the late 1960s and early '70s before the return of paper destination labels affixed to the door windows. *Les Riley*

In the late 1960s the 'Westerns', in common with other classes of diesel locomotive, began to emerge from overhaul in BR's new corporate livery of Rail blue. Thus adorned, No D1073 *Western Bulwark*, the highest-numbered example of its class and then just over five years old, passes Aller Junction in June 1969 with the St Austell–Kensington Olympia Motorail service. At the time of writing there are no such services running in the UK, but, with the price of fuel approaching £6 per gallon, the concept of transporting 40 or more cars on a single train travelling to/from the heart of the holiday area (be it Cornwall, the Lakes or Scotland) seems ever more sensible. *Les Riley*

The 'English Riviera' resorts of Torquay, Paignton and Brixham have always enjoyed a decent rail service to and from London; indeed, the eight-mile stretch of line between Newton Abbot and Paignton (always known locally as 'the branch'), with stations at Torre and Torquay, enjoyed a pretty good service to all parts of the UK. Reference to a 1970s Western Region timetable reveals daily services from Paignton and Torquay to London, Birmingham and Leeds (the 'Devonian'). These were augmented during the high season, and on summer Saturdays Liverpool, Newcastle, Manchester and Cardiff could all be reached direct. Here, on 14 June 1969, a Paignton–Paddington service is pictured calling at Torquay behind No D1017 *Western Warrior*. Adding character are a Morris Traveller estate car parked on the station forecourt (right) and the rusty sidings in the foreground. *Les Riley*

Working hard and no doubt making a great deal of 'Maybach music', a maroon-liveried 'Western' (believed to be No D1069 *Western Vanguard*, though this is not confirmed) passes Tre-groes Moor as it tackles the steeply graded single-line section between Fishguard Harbour and Manorowen signalbox, a distance of some 3½ miles at a ruling gradient of 1 in 50. The train consists of empty stock (from an excursion to Fishguard Harbour) returning to the carriage sidings at Landore, Swansea, some 71 miles away. The photograph was taken on 23 May 1970. *John Spencer Gilks*

Reading has always been a very important point on Britain's rail network, being, *inter alia*, a 'border town' where the Southern Region and Western Region met. Reinforcing the point is this photograph taken on 20 July 1970 at Reading General station. On the right, waiting to depart from Platform 5, is No D1041 *Western Prince* at the head of a Bristol–Paddington express; alongside is a Class 123 'Inter-City' DMU forming a Paddington–Oxford semi-fast service, while on the far left is an ageing EMU used on the SR to/from Waterloo. *Author*

Completed at Swindon in April 1962, No D1003 *Western Pioneer* was one of seven early examples that appeared first in green livery. By now repainted blue, it is pictured here at Westbury station in August 1970 in charge of a Paignton–Paddington service. Dominating the scene is the GWR Westbury North signalbox (left), since demolished following the introduction of more modern signalling. Many such signalboxes have been swept away, but a similar 'box at Totnes survives, albeit as the station buffet! *Derek Cross*

Above: No D1049 *Western Monarch* is pictured on 21 August 1970 ambling along the single line that once formed part of the Cheddar Valley route but has latterly become known as the Merehead branch (and continues to provide access to the major quarry operations at Merehead, operated by Foster Yeoman). The photograph was taken at Wanstrow, a small village midway between Shepton Mallet and Frome, on the eastern edge of the Mendips. Wanstrow has been a settlement since Roman times and is mentioned in the Domesday Book. The train appears to be transporting railway ballast (rather than stone for a commercial customer) and is on its way to join the main line at East Somerset Junction, between Frome and Bruton. *Derek Cross*

Left: The summer of 1970 saw construction of a short stretch of new line linking the quarry complex at Merehead with the erstwhile Cheddar Valley line, by now truncated at Cranmore. No D1041 *Western Prince* is seen cautiously propelling a stone train on 14 August. Note that, to facilitate the move, a brake van has been provided at each end of the train. *Ivo Peters*

Hydraulic heaven at Westbury station on 22 August 1970. Standing at the platform is 'Hymek' No D7014, at the head of a passenger train (1V28) from Weymouth to Bristol, while passing on its way to the sidings at Westbury depot is No D1035 *Western Yeoman*. Besides emphasising the large number of grilles associated with the 'Western' class, the photograph gives prominence to the nameplate. Little thought can have been given to its value at the time, but in the intervening years the price of such items has increased dramatically, to the extent that in 2011 a single plate from a sister locomotive sold for around £10,000. Interestingly the identity of *Western Yeoman* has been perpetuated in preservation, despite the fact that the locomotive itself was scrapped in 1976. This apparent conundrum is explained by the fact that sister No D1010 was preserved by Foster Yeoman Ltd, which, for reasons that will be obvious, had it restored as No D1035. *Derek Cross*

In charge of a Saturdays-only summer-dated service from Minehead direct through to Paddington, No D1014 *Western Leviathan* is pictured passing Clink Road Junction near Frome (the line from which can be seen on the right, beyond the second and third carriages) on 22 August 1970. Released to traffic in December 1962, the locomotive had been allocated initially to Cardiff Canton shed and was destined to remain in service until August 1974, when it was withdrawn from Plymouth Laira; the end came six months later, in February 1975, when it was scrapped at BREL Swindon. *Derek Cross*

It is easy to forget that at one time Somerset had an extensive coalfield and numerous collieries. For many years the coal mined around Radstock was taken away via the Somerset & Dorset line to Bath and Bristol, but following closure of the S&D in March 1966 greater use was made of the GWR branch to Radstock. Pictured near Mells on said branch is No D1023 *Western Fusilier* (since preserved) at the head of a long rake of coal empties from Portishead power station. The photograph was taken on 28 April 1971, on which day the other loaded coal train from Radstock to Portishead was hauled by 'Warship' No D823 *Hermes*. *Ivo Peters*

Photographed from a DMU (on which the author had travelled from Cardiff), class doyen No D1000 *Western Enterprise* runs light-engine into the station at Carmarthen on 5 August 1971. At this time a significant quantity of milk was still being transported by rail from West Wales (and Cornwall) to London. By now the former through route to Aberystwyth had been truncated a little way to the north of Lampeter, and it was the milk traffic, specifically from the large creamery at Felin Fach, on the erstwhile Aberayron branch, that was keeping the line open; no doubt *Western Enterprise* had been up there with milk empties from Acton and was now heading back to the holding sidings at Carmarthen before returning to the creamery to collect a train of loaded six-wheel milk tanks for the overnight trip to London, a journey of some 230 miles. The remaining stretch of line north of Carmarthen was destined to close a couple of years later, in 1973. *Author*

Above: Wednesday 14 June 1972 finds No D1048 *Western Lady* creeping past the signalbox at Clink Road Junction, northeast of Frome, with a long rake of stone empties bound for nearby Merehead Quarry. Stone traffic still plays a major part in rail-freight operations in and around Westbury, although the trains of today are longer (and faster) than that seen here. *Derek Cross*

Right: Calling at Swindon on the glorious afternoon of 19 June 1972, No D1041 *Western Prince* makes its first stop since departing Paddington with the 17.12 for Weston-super-Mare. Following further stops at Bristol Parkway, Bristol Temple Meads and Yatton, the train was scheduled to reach its destination at 19.38 – a total journey time of 2hr 26min for a distance of 137 miles, giving an average speed of 56mph. Travelling behind *Western Prince* in a train of blue-and-grey coaches is something that should again be possible once the locomotive, nowadays preserved on the East Lancashire Railway, returns to traffic in a couple of years' time. *Author*

Above: In March 1973 the second man looks back from of the cab of No D1050 *Western Ruler*, about to set off from Bristol Temple Meads with a train of empty stock bound for Malago Vale carriage sidings, located on the down side of the WR main line between the local stations of Bedminster and Parson Street. On the right of the picture can be seen the signalbox that controlled the entrance to the large diesel depot at Bristol Bath Road. This has now closed, and all traces of both signalbox and depot have entirely disappeared. *Western Ruler* similarly is no more; built at Crewe and placed in traffic from Cardiff Canton in January 1963, it was destined to be withdrawn from Plymouth Laira in April 1975, after a working life of just 12 years. *Derek Cross*

Right: The date is 26 April 1973, and spring and its associated blossoms are well underway as No D1071 *Western Renown* heads an up train through Sydney Gardens, that wonderful oasis of calm situated close to the centre of Bath (and established as long ago as 1795). No doubt motivated by health and safety considerations, Network Rail has recently announced its intention to fence off the line here; some consolation lies in the fact that the railings will be of Georgian or Victorian palisade style, but one wonders whether they are necessary at all, given that the railway has run quite happily through the gardens since the 1840s. *Ivo Peters*

27

Left: A classic view of Bristol Temple Meads, with No D1050 *Western Ruler* waiting to depart with an Inter-City service for Paddington on 17 May 1973. One of the more camera-shy members of its class, this locomotive by now had less than two years left in service, being withdrawn from Plymouth Laira in April 1975. *Derek Cross*

Right: Blue-liveried No D1047 *Western Lord* arrives at Bristol Temple Meads in May 1973 with a train from Weymouth. Also present are two Brush-built locomotives still in BR green – Class 31 No 5654 and, partially visible on the right of the picture, Class 47 No 1921. Built at Crewe and placed in traffic from Cardiff Canton in February 1963, *Western Lord* was destined to be withdrawn from Laira 13 years later and scrapped at Swindon in September 1976, but coincidentally both the diesel-electrics survive today – the '47' in preservation on the Battlefield Line in Leicestershire as No 47 640 and the '31' (despite being older than the 'Western', having been completed in September 1960) still in main-line service as No 31 454. *Derek Cross*

Above: On 18 August 1973 No D1053 *Western Patriarch* rounds the curve at Grafton East Junction, 1½ miles from Savernake, with the down 'Cornish Riviera Express'. Having left London at 11.30, the train was scheduled to make its first stop at Exeter St Davids, 173 miles from Paddington, at 13.53. Then, as now, the WR main line to the West was 'high speed' as far as Exeter but much less so thereafter, the remaining 132 miles of the journey to Penzance taking a further three hours. *John Spencer Gilks*

Right: Some 202 miles from Paddington, No D1007 *Western Talisman* reaches journey's end as it draws into the platform at Paignton on 19 August 1973. In earlier times the train would have continued as far as Kingswear (for Dartmouth), along a further 6½ miles of steeply graded single line, but by now the BR section ended here; the line onward to Kingswear was already in private hands, and on this day the steam locomotive providing the connecting service was none other than LNER 'A3' Pacific *Flying Scotsman*. *Author*

No D1058 *Western Nobleman* awaits the 'right away' from the east end of Exeter St Davids station with a Plymouth-Paddington service in September 1973. The next stop will be Taunton, and overall journey time 2¾ hours for the 173-mile journey to London. The array of semaphore signals, signalbox and NCL depot (note the yellow sign visible above the locomotive) all recall a bygone era. *Author*

Saturday 29 September 1973 finds No D1023 *Western Fusilier* train arriving at Exeter with a Paddington–Penzance service; the headcode is most definitely wrong and should read '1B39'. The train has just passed over the very wide level crossing immediately east of the station where, still to this day, road traffic builds up quickly. In those days there were an incredible 18 trains from Paddington to the West Country on high summer Saturdays; Penzance, Paignton, Newquay and Barnstaple were all served direct, with some trains running direct from Paddington to first stop Totnes or first stop Dawlish. Destined to be among the last 'Westerns' in service, finally succumbing to withdrawal in February 1977, No D1023 is now preserved as part of the National Collection at York. *Author*

Exeter St Davids was always a good place to watch/chase/photograph 'Westerns', which could appear on expresses to/from London and inter-regional services to/from Bristol, as well as on freight trains and also resting between duties or undergoing an exam at the Fuel & Inspection point, on the site of the old steam shed. A regular 'Western' turn was train 1A59, a Plymouth-Paddington express, with which No D1058 *Western Nobleman* is seen ready to depart, about an hour and a quarter after leaving Plymouth, on Saturday 29 September 1973. Following withdrawal in January 1977 this locomotive would become the last 'Western' to be cut up at Swindon, in June 1979. *Author*

A classic scene at Exeter St Davids as No D1047 *Western Lord* awaits departure from Platform 1 with a very long, perhaps strengthened train forming the 12.26 Paddington–Penzance. In the 1970s Exeter was a very interesting place in railway terms, for in addition to the aforementioned WR, SR and inter-regional passenger services there was a much higher level of commercial freight traffic; a 1973 notebook records examples of Classes 08, 25, 31, 33, 35, 45, 46, 47 and 52 being observed on just one day! *Author*

Left: Just east of Reading the Great Western main line passes through the famous Brunel-designed earthwork known as Sonning Cutting, which location has long been popular with photographers. Pictured at the western end of the cutting is No D1072 *Western Glory*, hauling a Class 8 mixed freight typical of the period but here, unusually, on the fast line. The photograph was taken in April 1974, by which time the locomotive had been in service for just over 10 years; turned out by Crewe Works in November 1963 as the penultimate locomotive numerically, it was nevertheless followed into traffic by a number of others with lower numbers, the last of these being Swindon-built No D1029 *Western Legionnaire*. *I. J. Hodson*

Below: It was E. M. Forster who said: 'Railway termini: they are our gates to the glorious and the unknown. Through them we pass out into adventure and sunshine, to them, alas! we return.' We can be pretty certain that this was not written from the perspective of a railway enthusiast, but it could very well be applied to Paddington in the 1970s. It is certainly an interesting location for taking photographs, made all the more challenging by the huge roof and the curvature of the line. Here, on 20 May 1974, 'Westerns' Nos D1014 *Western Leviathan* and D1059 *Western Empire* flank Class 47/4 No 47 479 as all three await departure with trains for the Midlands and the West. *Author*

No D1070 *Western Gauntlet* arrives at Paddington in June 1974 with a train from Worcester. The journey would have been a leisurely one, the distance of 120 miles taking 2hr 32min. Of the seven daily through trains from Worcester, some of which originated from Hereford, two offered full dining service – as the timetable stated, 'According to the time of day Breakfast, Lunch, Afternoon Tea, High Tea or Dinner is served'; the others offered 'A buffet service of light refreshments and drinks'. *Author*

Passing the signalbox at Clink Road Junction, No D1008 *Western Harrier* heads west with the down 'Cornish Riviera Express' in June 1974. The GWR signal in the 'off' position on the right of the picture indicates that the train will be taking the Frome avoiding line, thereby speeding the passengers' journey to the West Country but depriving them of the sight of the town's attractive wooden station; the other signal protects that line into Frome. *Derek Cross*

With the tide coming in along the famous sea wall at Dawlish a family appear to have left the beach to watch the passage of No D1039 *Western King*, heading west with an excursion train (1Z74) bound for the 'English Riviera' at Paignton in June 1974. In the distance can be seen Langstone Rock, favoured by photographers as a vantage-point for recording trains heading in the opposite direction along this very scenic stretch of line. *Derek Cross*

The arrival on the Western Region of the English Electric-built Class 50s, displaced from the West Coast main line by the completion of electrification, signalled the beginning of the end for the 'Westerns'. Pictured at Newton Abbot in June 1974 is the as yet unnamed No 50 026, on a crew-training run between Plymouth and Exeter. On the platform road and about to overtake the special a Plymouth–Paddington express is headed by No D1072 *Western Glory*. Nothing, however, lasts forever, and No 50 026 would itself be withdrawn in December 1990, 14 years after the 'Western', which succumbed in November 1976. *Derek Cross*

Photographed on 10 June 1974, a Penzance–Paddington express headed by No D1035 *Western Yeoman* coasts past Aller Junction. It was here that the lines to/from Paignton and Kingswear (seen on the left) joined the main line; more recently, however, the connection has been moved closer to Newton Abbot, such that this location is no longer Aller Junction and is known instead as Aller divergence! What would I. K. Brunel – or, for that matter, Derek Cross – have said? *Derek Cross*

Before the near-universal adoption of multiple units, railway termini were busy places, with coaching stock, parcels vans and sometimes mail vans being shunted around, often to release locomotives from incoming trains. Pictured at Penzance on 13 June 1974 are 'Westerns' Nos D1036 *Western Emperor* and D1012 *Western Firebrand*. Overlooking proceedings is the Hotel Royale in Chyandour Cliff Road – subsequently converted to apartments, with stunning views of Mount's Bay. *Derek Cross*

The crack train serving the far South West has for years been the 'Cornish Riviera Express'. Introduced by the GWR as long ago as July 1906, this still appears as a named train in today's timetable but runs without a headboard. As long ago as 1974 any sort of 'specialness' had clearly gone, witness this view of a filthy No D1030 *Western Musketeer* drawing into the platform at Truro *en route* from Penzance to Paddington on 13 June. Despite its appalling external condition it was destined to remain in traffic for almost two more years, finally being withdrawn in April 1976. *Derek Cross*

During the course of his journey from Penzance to Bristol behind Nos D1006 and D1012 Derek took the opportunity to record this view of Brunel's Royal Albert Bridge across the River Tamar at Saltash. As proudly proclaimed on the bridge itself, it had been built in 1859 and was thus already 115 years old when photographed in June 1974. Unusually, the Saltash bridge is one of the few structures best photographed from the train, as opposed to any surrounding location. The Tamar forms the border between Devon and Cornwall. *Derek Cross*

By 16.04 Derek's train had reached Plymouth North Road, where the pilot engine, No D1006, would be detached and in all likelihood proceed to Laira depot, leaving No D1012 to continue alone to Bristol. On the left of the picture, beyond one of the distinctive clocks that for so long characterised this station, is a third 'Western', No D1068 *Western Reliance*, awaiting departure with a northbound parcels train. *Derek Cross*

On 29 July 1974 No D1033 *Western Trooper* races through Dawlish station with the 06.30 service from Penzance to Paddington. Built at Crewe, this locomotive had been among the last to enter service, being placed in traffic from Old Oak Common in January 1964, and was destined to be among the later examples withdrawn, from Laira at the end of September 1976. Along with sister No D1034 it was to see further use as a steam-heating unit, thereby cheating the scrapman until May 1979. *Author*

In charge of a westbound stone train originating from the Southern Region, an immaculate No D1034 *Western Dragoon* pauses on the centre road at Reading to await the passage of a Paddington–Swansea express, hauled by a Class 47. The final Crewe-built 'Western' and the penultimate member of the class to be placed in traffic, on 15 April 1964, *Western Dragoon* was nevertheless destined to remain in service only until October 1975. Note that by the time of this photograph, taken in July 1974, the embossed 'D' on the number plate has been overpainted black, reflecting the decision, following the end of main-line BR steam, to drop this prefix for diesel locomotives; with painted numbers or transfers it was an easy change to effect, but with cast plates it was clearly much more difficult. *I. J. Hodson*

Photographed on 17 August 1974, No D1029 *Western Legionnaire* approaches Reading General at the head of an express for South Wales. The last of its class to emerge from Swindon Works, in July 1964, it was to have a very short working life – even by 'Western' standards – of barely 10 years, being withdrawn in November 1974, just three months after the photograph was taken. Interestingly, this locomotive had been subjected to a minor name change in September 1967, when (somewhat belatedly, it must be said) it was realised that on the original nameplates 'Legionnaire' had been spelt with only one 'n'. *Author*

A very dramatic picture, taken in September 1974, featuring No D1028 *Western Hussar* racing a thunderstorm near Twyford. The train is the 14.30 express from Paddington to Paignton, with only Sonning Cutting to negotiate before making its first stop at Reading. Placed in traffic on 29 February 1964, this locomotive would remain active until 5 October 1976, during its career reportedly covering some 1,256,000 miles. Although this figure was bettered by No D1005 *Western Venturer* (see page 72), it should be borne in mind that the latter was active for nearly two years longer. Purists will doubtless be pleased that both locomotives were built at Swindon! *I. J. Hodson*

No D1023 *Western Fusilier* stands light-engine at the end of Paddington's Platform 1 as No D1049 *Western Monarch* arrives at Platform 2 with an express from Plymouth; by contrast *Western Fusilier* would appear to have arrived on an inter-regional working from Birmingham New Street. Taken in September 1974, the picture highlights some of the detail differences between individual locomotives: *Western Fusilier* has two clasps for a headboard, whilst *Western Monarch* has a plain front. It had been thought that locomotives with an additional cab-ventilation flap (among them No D1028 in the previous picture) were those lacking the clasps, but research for this book has revealed that Nos D1003/5/25-8/40/6/9/65/71 were all without clasps at one time. *I. J. Hodson*

The distinctive half-timbered building beside the railway (right) identifies the location for this picture as Cowley Bridge Junction, a mile or so to the north of Exeter St Davids. The single-track Barnstaple branch can be seen curving away to the left as an unidentified 'Western' passes with a Paddington–Plymouth express on 26 September 1974. Subsequently the trees here would become overgrown, obscuring the view, but in recent years major surgery has been carried out, with the result that photographs such as this are once again possible. *John Spencer Gilks*

Left: Headed by No D1043 *Western Duke*, a Penzance–Paddington service crosses the Class A viaduct at St Stephen's Coombe, a few miles west of St Austell, on 29 September 1974. Some 738ft long and 70ft high, this was opened in 1886, replacing an earlier timber structure (one of numerous examples built by the Cornwall Railway), the stone piers for which, by now overgrown, can be seen on the left of the picture. *John Spencer Gilks*

Right: Relics of the GWR in the form of a lower-quadrant signal and 'Catch Points' board in typical GWR typeface (right) add character to this picture of No D1068 *Western Reliance* approaching Bodmin Road with the northbound 'Cornishman' 10.25 Penzance–Leeds) on 21 October 1974. The locomotive is displaying an incorrect headcode, which should be 1E21; by now photographers were frequently faced with a dilemma over whether to believe the timetable or what the locomotive was showing, and it came as no surprise when, a year or so later, the use of headcode displays was abandoned. *Derek Cross*

Shadows lengthen on the afternoon of 21 October 1974 as No D1055 *Western Advocate* runs through Lostwithiel station with the down 'Cornish Riviera Express'. This part of Cornwall is noted for the production of china clay, witness the long rake of such wagons (right) coated liberally with china-clay dust. *Western Advocate* would remain in service until January 1976, ultimately being scrapped at Swindon six months later. *Derek Cross*

In 1974 'Westerns' ruled in Cornwall! In this photograph, taken on 21 October, No D1042 *Western Princess* coasts into Lostwithiel with the down 'Cornishman' (07.35 Leeds–Penzance) as the afternoon St Erth–Acton milk train heads north behind No D1047 *Western Lord*. Judging from the white deposits on its roof this locomotive had been engaged on china-clay workings earlier in the week and was perhaps returning to its home depot of Plymouth Laira for an exam and a clean. *Derek Cross*

The Royal Hotel stands guard over Par station as No D1010 *Western Campaigner* drifts to a halt with a Paddington–Penzance express in October 1974. After leaving Par the train will tackle the 1-in-60 climb to St Austell, its next stop, before coasting downhill again towards Truro; such is the nature of the Cornish main line! Lighter duties on the West Somerset Railway now occupy this Swindon-built locomotive, which in October 2012 celebrates its 50th birthday. *Derek Cross*

On 27 October 1974, just 45 miles into its journey from Penzance and with 260 still to go before reaching Paddington, No D1044 *Western Duchess* calls at Par with the up 'Cornish Riviera Express', which at this time had an end-to-end journey time of 5hr 10min. In the background can be seen a Metro-Cammell DMU stabled between duties on the Newquay branch. Less than a mile from Par station was the diesel depot at St Blazey, where 'Westerns' would congregate at the GWR roundhouse (still extant today) and where, for the 1971 depot open day, No D1020 *Western Hero* was infamously presented to the public in filthy condition – a reminder that these locomotives, despite being used primarily on passenger trains, put in much valuable work hauling freight traffic, most notably milk and china clay in Cornwall. *Derek Cross*

Left: No D1021 *Western Cavalier* pictured in close-up at Old Oak Common depot in West London on 18 November 1974, the puff of smoke from its roof suggesting the locomotive has just been started up following maintenance at 'the factory'. The photograph goes a long way toward confirming the belief, held by many photographers, that bright autumn sunshine produces the most rewarding results. *I. J. Hodson*

Right: With No D1058 *Western Nobleman* at its head, a westbound parcels train awaits departure from Newport on a misty morning in March 1975, its likely destination Cardiff or possibly Swansea. The yellow NCL (National Carriers Ltd) van on the right serves as a reminder that, during the BR era, a proportion of Britain's road-haulage industry was also under state control. Today, at almost precisely this location, is a new footbridge, completed in 2010 as part of a major station redevelopment; bearing a startling resemblance to a spaceship, it is deemed by some to be of 'iconic' design, although the local newspaper has been inundated with complaints about it! *Les Riley*

Reaffirming that 'Westerns' on freight traffic were not uncommon, No D1028 *Western Hussar* sets off from Westbury yard with a train of empty coal hoppers returning to South Wales. Photographed on 22 March 1975, the locomotive would remain in traffic for a further 18 months, being withdrawn (from Laira) in October 1976 but thereafter lingering at Swindon to become one of the last two 'Westerns' to be scrapped, in June 1979. *Les Riley*

Passing the large goods yard (left) and the locomotive depot and sidings (right), No D1048 *Western Lady* approaches the station at Westbury with the 09.55 Paignton–Paddington on 22 March 1975. Not all trains pass through the station, as Westbury, like Frome, has an avoiding line, in this case from Heywood Road Junction to Fairwood Junction – a distance of just over two miles. The locomotive depot here has now closed, but the extensive yards remain open, concerned mainly with stone traffic and infrastructure traffic for Network Rail. *Les Riley*

Right: A fine picture of an unidentified 'Western' racing westwards near Aldermaston with the 11.30 Paddington–Penzance, better known as the down 'Cornish Riviera Express'. Just under 45 miles from Paddington, Aldermaston is on a very gentle climb from Reading all the way to Savernake, a distance of about 35 miles, the steepest part of which is two miles at 1 in 200. In August 1975, when the photograph was taken, it had some sidings (used in connection with stone traffic from Westbury) and a loop; at that time, however, it was more famous as the home of the Atomic Weapons Research Establishment, and in the years that followed it featured regularly in the news on account of the CND demonstrations that were held there.
John Spencer Gilks

Below: Between Taunton and Reading the railway passes through the counties of Somerset, Wiltshire and Berkshire, and away from Frome and Westbury and the emerging commuter towns to the east of Reading the landscape is largely agricultural. Pictured heading west past the site of Grafton East Junction on 9 August 1975 is the 07.53 Paignton–Paddington, headed by an unidentified 'Western'. Just under 70 miles from Paddington, the junction was to the little-used spur to the MSWJR. On the left, the former bridge abutments across the Kennett and Avon canal can be seen behind the platelayers' hut. *John Spencer Gilks*

Early on the morning of 30 August 1975, and barely a month before withdrawal, No D1025 *Western Guardsman* approaches Dawlish station with the 07.53 Paignton–Paddington. Photography at Dawlish was great fun (when the sun was out) but was not without its problems: the author and his father often stayed in the hotel seen on the right of the picture, and co-ordinating breakfast with photography could present a challenge if the train were a couple of minutes early or service in the hotel a little on the slow side! *Les Riley*

Above: Towards the end of the 'Western' era a series of railtours visited various parts of the WR, perhaps the most famous being the legendary 'Western China Clay Farewell' tour of Cornwall on 4 December 1976. Prior to this, however, the Wirral Railway Circle tour had arranged the 'Pembroke Coast Express', run on 25 October 1975, when the author and his father enjoyed a memorable day travelling around West Wales behind No D1013 *Western Ranger*, pictured here at Pembroke Dock station. Some say that it was railtours such as this that revitalised the enthusiast market; this was only seven years after the end of steam, and a number of people who had lost interest in railways at that time were moved to reconsider when they realised that the diesel-hydraulics too were about to be consigned to history. *Derek Cross*

Right: On 27 March 1976 No D1053 *Western Patriarch* pulls away from the Oxford stop with the 12.25 Birmingham New Street–Paddington. Note that by now the headcode boxes on the 'Westerns' were being used to display the locomotive number instead of the train's reporting number – a boon for photographers! Placed in traffic from Old Oak Common in February 1963, *Western Patriarch* would remain in traffic for just nine months after this photograph was taken, being withdrawn from Laira in December 1976. *Author*

No D1033 *Western Trooper* accelerates away from the Newport stop with train 1Z47, the 13.55 relief service from Cardiff to Paddington; in a minute it will cross the River Usk as it heads east towards the Severn Tunnel. The photograph was taken on 20 April 1976, at which time the 133-mile journey would have taken a shade over two hours. *Western Trooper* had just five months left in service. *Les Riley*

Right: A fine study of No D1051 *Western Ambassador* standing at the platform at Reading General on a fine sunny day in April 1976 with the 1V38 12.25 Birmingham New Street–Paddington; from here the train will run non-stop to its destination, just 36 miles away, and it is entirely likely that on this stretch the locomotive will attain its maximum speed of 90mph. The photograph also makes for an interesting comparison with that on page 11, showing the locomotive in broadly original condition. Built at Crewe and placed in traffic from Cardiff Canton depot in January 1963, *Western Ambassador* would be withdrawn from Plymouth Laira in September 1976 and scrapped at Swindon in August 1977. *Les Riley*

Left: In the 1970s, in common with Crewe, Doncaster and various other significant railway centres, Reading General played host to a significant number of enthusiasts, particularly on Saturdays. Such was the case on 24 April 1976, when there must be at least two dozen 'spotters' at the west end of the up platform (4). The object of their interest is No D1005 *Western Venturer*, seen here on a down platform about to set off westwards with a relief service from Paddington to Plymouth, just over 189 miles distant. *Les Riley*

Pictured in glorious conditions on the evening of 29 May 1976, No D1070 *Western Gauntlet* heads west at Sheldon Bridge near Teignmouth towards its next stop at Newton Abbot with train 1B83, the 15.30 Paddington–Penzance. Having already covered some 189 miles, it has a further 116 to go before reaching its destination. The locomotive would be withdrawn at the end of the year, its last day of service being 30 December 1976. *Les Riley*

The author offers no apologies for the number of pictures taken between Teignmouth and Dawlish Warren, on what has always been a highly photogenic stretch of railway line. Seen from Langstone Rock – long a favourite location among photographers – on 21 August 1976 is train 1B15, the 08.30 Paddington–Plymouth, headed by No D1068 *Western Reliance*, the latter looking (and, apparently, working) well for a locomotive destined to be withdrawn just six weeks later. The clothing of the people walking along the sea wall reminds us that this was a beautifully hot day, one of many in a famously hot summer. *Les Riley*

On summer Saturdays in the 1970s, Cornwall saw an abundance of holiday trains. Here, on 28 August 1976, No D1072 *Western Glory* is approaching the long-closed station at St Blazey with train 1A15, the Saturdays-only summer-dated 10.30 service from Newquay to Paddington, which will join the main line at Par. This locomotive would remain in traffic for just three more months, being withdrawn from Plymouth Laira in November 1976 and cut up at Swindon Works in April 1977. Newquay still sees summer-dated extra trains to/from London and also the North of England, worked nowadays by the seemingly evergreen High Speed Trains. *Les Riley*

On Sunday 29 August 1976 No D1010 *Western Campaigner* approaches St Austell with train 5B79, the 09.45 empty-stock working from Par to Penzance. That 1976 was the year of the very hot summer is confirmed by the state of the lineside vegetation, much of which is almost brown in colour, while the semaphore signals, the platelayer's hut, the pristine permanent way and the tidy yard (subsequently developed as a housing estate) combine to give an accurate flavour of the Western Region at this time. Destined to be withdrawn in February 1977, after less than 15 years in BR service, *Western Campaigner* would go on to enjoy an active second career on the West Somerset Railway (see page 74). *Author*

Sunday 29 August 1976 finds No D1041 *Western Prince* creeping into St Austell station with train 5B14, the 12.55 Penzance–Plymouth Laira Sidings, consisting of empty stock (from a special to Penzance earlier in the day) returning to the carriage shed at Laira for servicing. As explained earlier, a number of 'Westerns' had by this time had their headcode boxes set to display the locomotive number (something to which they were ideally suited, given that the second digit was always a '0'), but here something appears to have gone awry, '0041' providing only a clue as to the identity of the locomotive. Coincidentally, *Western Prince* is another of the preserved examples, being based nowadays on the East Lancashire Railway, where it recently lent one of its engines to a 'Hymek' (No D7076) to keep the latter in service – a welcome display of 21st-century hydraulic solidarity! *Author*

Piloting trains over the banks in Devon and Cornwall was commonplace in steam days but less so after diesels took over, and photographs of 'Westerns' double-heading with other classes (they could not work in multiple) are few and far between, hence the inclusion of this picture. On a very wet 30 August 1976, the 1B81 08.13 Bristol–Penzance had been making slow progress behind No D1028 *Western Hussar*, and at some stage Class 25/2 No 25 217 was added to provide assistance, the unusual combination being seen here departing St Austell. Whether as a result of its ailment on this day is unknown, but *Western Hussar* was destined to be withdrawn from service just six weeks later. *Author*

Train 6A21, the 16.40 St Erth–Acton milk churns, sets off at the start of its journey behind No D1048 *Western Lady* on a damp 30 August 1976. The laden milk train departed for London – some 295 miles away – each afternoon, the empties beginning their return journey from the capital at 03.13 the following day. The tanks themselves – glass-lined six-wheelers designed specifically for transporting milk – have long since disappeared from the rail network, the last of the WR milk trains having ceased running in the 1980s, but a few examples (emblazoned with the logos of such well-known brands as St Ivel, Unigate and United Dairies) survive in preservation, as does *Western Lady* (see page 75). *Author*

On Monday 30 August 1976 No D1051 *Western Ambassador* draws into the station at Liskeard with the 09.30 Padddington–Penzance as, on the opposite platform, would-be passengers await an up train. Some 243 miles from Paddington, Liskeard is the junction station for Looe, nine miles distant. Services on this single-line branch (seen curving off to the left) use a separate platform that is just out of view. The area around Liskeard has long been popular with photographers, being noted for its viaducts, of which probably the best known is Moorswater, about a mile to the west, from where the line climbs as far as Doublebois before beginning its descent to Bodmin Parkway (formerly Bodmin Road). *Author*

China clay has long constituted a significant proportion of rail-borne freight in Cornwall. Here train 6B71, the 11.26 clay hood empties from Carne Point (on the Fowey Branch) to Burngullow, passes through St Austell station on 31 August 1976 behind No D1013 *Western Ranger*, unusually with red-backed name and number plates. By now the locomotive had just six months left in BR service, withdrawal following in February 1977, but the line to Carne Point remains open for china-clay traffic, transported in longer trains of modified Merry Go Round hoppers known as CDAs, hauled by Class 66 locomotives. *Les Riley*

On 31 August 1976 No D1013 is seen heading east, about to pass through St Austell station with train 6B71, the china-clay train from Burngullow to Fowey. Destined to be among those 'Westerns' that escaped the scrapman's torch, No D1013 is nowadays owned by the Western Locomotive Association and based on the Severn Valley Railway but at the time of writing, is out of service, its cooler groups, electrical frames and ancillary equipment having been removed for extensive maintenance and cleaning. Also owned by the WLA (and based at the same location) is sister locomotive No D1062 *Western Courier*, which remains in traffic, albeit working on only one engine. *Author*

Left: A sad picture, but one that is very much part of the 'Western' story. Aside from seven that would be saved for posterity, all members of the class were scrapped at Swindon Works, where on 25 May 1977 No D1005 *Western Venturer*, by now nameless and reduced to little more than a shell, is seen awaiting its fate. This was the highest-mileage 'Western', having covered just under 1.4 million miles between entering service in June 1962 and withdrawal in November 1976. The end would come barely a week after the photograph was taken. *Author*

Below: Another view at Swindon Works, recorded on the same day and featuring Nos D1025 *Western Guardsman* and D1001 *Western Pathfinder*, by now shorn of their nameplates and cabside numbers. Swindon was, of course, famous for locomotive construction but was also responsible for scrapping large numbers, including nearly 800 diesels, of which more than 200 were hydraulics – prompting contemporary magazine headlines such as 'GWR: Gone With Regret' and 'Hydraulic Holocaust'. Less than 10 years after this photograph was taken, the works, which at its height had covered 300 acres and employed more than 14,000 people, would itself become a victim, closing in March 1986. Most of the buildings have since been demolished, but some have been retained to house the Steam Museum, plus the inevitable 'retail centre'; however, the latter is itself not without railway interest, for on the occasion of the author's most recent visit, in 2011, a GWR steam locomotive was to be found lurking amongst the shoppers! *Author*

May 1977 finds a sorry-looking No D1015 *Western Champion* keeping company with an immaculately restored 'Warship', No D821 *Greyhound*, at Swindon Works. Introduced to traffic in January 1963 from Cardiff Canton depot, the 'Western' had been withdrawn from Plymouth Laira in December 1976 but, despite its condition here, faced a brighter future than did its classmates on the preceding pages and, restored to its former glory, would one day return to the main line (see pages 78-80). Ironically both locomotives have now been in preservation for far longer than they were in BR service. *Author*

Seven 'Westerns' were saved for posterity. Among these was No D1010 *Western Campaigner*, which had originally been saved by Foster Yeoman Ltd and painted in green livery as No D1035 *Western Yeoman* for display on a plinth at the company's Merehead quarry. It was later restored to full working order at Didcot Railway Centre and, by now in the care of the Diesel & Electric Preservation Group, was moved in July 1991 to the West Somerset Railway, being seen here arriving at Blue Anchor on a service from Minehead. Displaying a test-train headcode, it is in the experimental 'desert sand' livery worn originally by No D1000 *Western Enterprise* and is fitted with the original-style cast BR emblems. Subsequent repaints would see the locomotive appear in green, blue and eventually its original maroon livery as No D1010. *Don Bishop*

Over the years a number of the surviving 'Westerns' have moved around from one preserved line to another. Following a spell on the Bodmin & Wenford Railway in Cornwall, No D1048 *Western Lady* has settled at the Midland Railway Centre in Derbyshire, being seen here in pristine condition at Swanwick Junction in April 1997, 20 years after withdrawal from Plymouth Laira depot. *Author*

Below: The locomotive that had for so long been masquerading as *Western Yeoman* finally regained its true identity in the early 1990s and, following a period in BR blue, has now been restored to maroon livery. Seen here with yellow buffer-beam, as applied to early locomotives prior to the introduction of the yellow warning panel, No D1010 *Western Campaigner* is pictured in July 2003 coasting downgrade towards Stogumber, on the West Somerset Railway, with a passenger train for Minehead. Until around 40 years ago this 25-mile branch from Taunton was, of course, WR territory, although by the time of the first 'Westerns' it was already in decline. Although a Butlins holiday camp was opened at Minehead in the early 1960s, traffic never really picked up and Dr Beeching had the line on his infamous list; freight went first, in 1964, and complete closure followed in 1971. However, just five years later the West Somerset Railway began serious operation between Minehead and Blue Anchor, from where the line was extended to Bishops Lydeard in 1979. Since then it has enjoyed great success, to the extent that it now carries around a quarter of a million passengers each year and stages frequent diesel galas, when passengers can sample the delights of 'Western' haulage. *Don Bishop*

Above: Although seemingly quite recent, this photograph, capturing a reunion around the turntable at Old Oak Common, was itself taken some years ago. The occasion was the open day staged at the famous West London depot on 6 August 2000, when all manner of locomotives were on display. Among more modern motive power were five diesel-hydraulics, all by now in preservation. From left to right are No D1015 *Western Champion*, 'Warship' No D821 *Greyhound*, D1023 *Western Fusilier*, 'Hymek' No D7076 and 'Warship' No D832 *Onslaught*. Sadly, the diesel depot and 'factory' at Old Oak Common have recently been demolished to make way for the Crossrail project. *Author*

On 16 June 2007 the sound of double-heading 'Westerns' was to be heard once again in Somerset, an excursion from Minehead (WSR) to Paddington having been organised to mark the 30th anniversary of the class's withdrawal by BR. Pictured near Bicknoller are Nos D1010 *Western Campaigner* (leading) and D1015 *Western Champion*, the train's apparently tautologous title an *homage* to the 'Western Requiem' railtour of 13 February 1977. Not being main-line-registered, No D1010 would be detached at Bishops Lydeard, leaving No D1015 to take the train forward to Taunton and ultimately Paddington. In recreating scenes such as this – not to mention tackling the logistics associated with running a train originating on a private line in the West of England and working through to London on the national network – the preservation movement deserves both thanks and all the support enthusiasts can offer. *Don Bishop*

Above: A recent trend amongst railway photographers has been to recreate as closely as possible pictures from a bygone age. This is a more demanding task than might at first be imagined, because, aside from the railway itself, the locomotive, the stock and the location may have changed too much. However, this superb photograph, taken on 7 April 2009 and featuring No D1015 *Western Champion* heading the 'Great Britain II' railtour alongside the sea wall at Dawlish *en route* to Penzance, captures a scene that could almost have been recorded 40 years earlier. At the time of writing the locomotive has been sidelined (see page 80), but hopefully it will soon be back in action, allowing more photographers the opportunity to record scenes such as this. *Don Bishop*

Right: Although when in BR service the 'Westerns' were largely confined to the Western Region, they could be found regularly on SR and LMR metals, particularly on freight trains in the London area, but they never ventured as far north as Scotland. However, with the return to the main line of No D1015 *Western Champion* that was to change: in the summer of 2008 the locomotive made an historic first visit to Edinburgh, and the following year saw it embark upon a more ambitious itinerary with the three-day 'Western Chieftain' railtour, which took it all the way to Kyle of Lochalsh. Taken on 19 June 2009, this photograph shows the special racing through Dunblane (incidentally a favourite Derek Cross location). *Bob Avery*

In 2010 *Western Champion* continued to visit locations unthinkable in BR days. It is seen here on 31 July storming out of Penrith *en route* to Carlisle with the 'Western Fellsrunner' railtour – its 50th since returning to the main line. Later that day it was to suffer a major engine failure, the necessary repairs putting it out of action for the whole of the 2011 season, but the Diesel Traction Group, which owns the locomotive, was hoping to have it back on the main line before too long. *Bob Avery*